POWER
IN THE
PADDOCK

POWER
IN THE
PADDOCK

A journey of healing and
transformation

Yolanda Sing

Chloé
CONSULTANTS PTY LTD

Published by CHLOE Consultants

www.chloeinsa.co.za

Power In The Paddock

ISBN 978-0-620-63304-8

First edition 2014

Copyright © 2014 Yolanda Sing

Cover design by Tim Hing

Photography by Werner Bentz

Editing by Rachel Bey-Miller

Book production by Quickfox Publishing

To my husband Jeff, and Erika, who have both touched, healed and transformed my life.

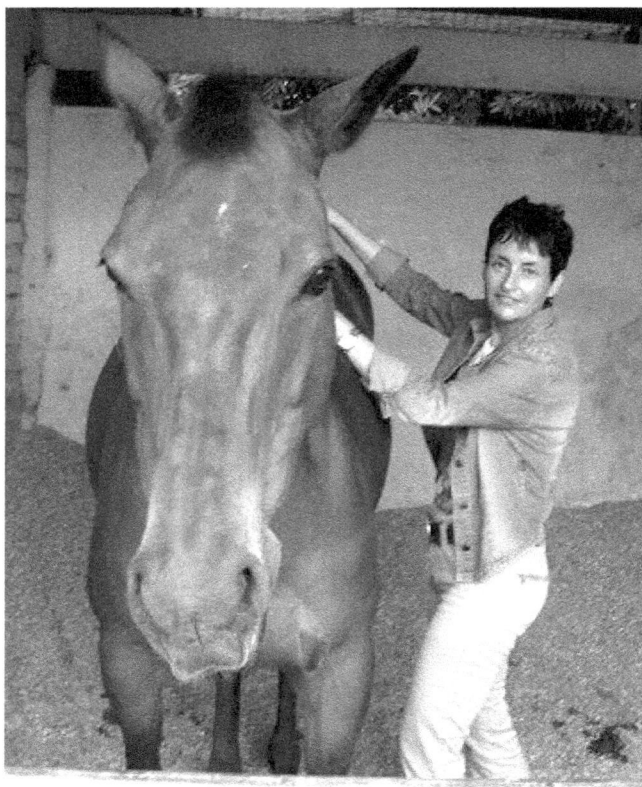

Erika and Yolanda just after the brain surgery, January 2007

INTRODUCTION

It took me many years to have the courage to write this book. Part of my reluctance was fear that people would look at me differently and treat me differently, if they knew that I was a brain tumor survivor. Part of it was fear that my words would not be powerful and that nobody would read my book.

But mostly, it was the pain of remembering.

I am not sure where the turning point was that liberated me to have the courage to tell the story, but here I am.

If my story inspires just one person, it was worth the risk.

If you are currently dealing with a life-challenging disease or are caught up in a career that does not inspire you, keep on reading. Even if neither of these categories applies to you, but you found this book in your hands, keep on reading because when the student is ready, the teacher appears.

Namasté

Yolanda Sing

꧁☙꧂

The Spirits speak

Since prehistoric times, humans have interacted with animals. Paintings on cave walls, hieroglyphics in Egyptian tombs, and remnants of ancient cultures across the world attest to this. This close association between our world and the animal kingdom survives to this day amongst indigenous peoples, who call on nature spirits for protection, healing and guidance. The Koi San of Africa revere the praying mantis, the Native Americans call upon their totem animals, and the Aborigines of Australia believe that the whales and dolphins sing the world into existence.

Animals have spoken to humans for centuries, acting as living connections to the realms of Spirit. In the words of Meister Eckhart (1260–1328), "Every creature is a word of God."

It is also said that the animals choose a person, not the other way around. The Horses chose Yolanda long before she arrived on this Physical Plane. It was a contract made between human and animal spirits, and the Gods blessed it.

Her contract was not an easy one because we knew that this would be her last reincarnation on the Physical Plane. The lessons that she signed up for would be challenging and only an old soul could qualify for them.

And we also knew that all the other lifetimes and reincarnations had prepared her for this journey, which would be her most powerful contribution to this world.

And so the journey began.

The kindergarten years

Born into a farmer's family in Elliot, a small town nestled between mountains on the southern tip of Africa, Yolanda's childhood years were happy and carefree. She loved being a farm girl — the open spaces, the fresh air, the animals and the Sun fed her soul.

Her first major life lesson was when she lost her biological mother in a car accident at the tender age of three months. This dramatic and painful event had a profound effect on shaping and preparing her for much bigger roles in life. As her Animal Spirit Guides, we knew that this event had been written in both their contracts; her departed mother's as well as her own. The lesson they needed to learn — to surrender to what is — came at a very high price.

She stayed with her grandparents until her father remarried when she was three years old.

We watched her struggle again when her father left the Physical Plane when she was a young girl of 18, leaving her without a male role model or a father figure. The pain and loss felt by her whole family was devastating, even for us observing their journey.

The familiar saying, "This too shall pass", which originated with Persian poets in the Middle Ages, came true, but not without leaving permanent scars on her psyche and those of her family.

The intervention

We, her Equine Animal Spirit Guides, knew what was written in her contract but she had to discover it for herself. Our sole purpose was to provide guidance and support along the way and to intervene only when it felt necessary. It was her journey to travel.

Her purpose in life, as with any other human being, was to discover her own unique soul purpose and to learn the lessons that she had signed up for during this lifetime.

All these life lessons are carefully constructed and agreed on before souls enter a physical body, only to be forgotten the minute they enter their mother's womb.

Later on, we watched how she slipped further and further away from her calling, by studying, climbing the corporate ladder and being caught up in the business world.

We also rejoiced when she met and married her soul partner, as we knew that this relationship was blessed and written in her contract. It was a relationship designed to teach her challenging lessons, primarily about ethnic differences, forgiveness and sustaining lifelong friendships.

As a true child of the world, she was eager to learn and discover what life had to offer and welcomed challenges to her own world views — views that changed constantly as her soul progressed.

We watched her manifest as a global jet setter, living the high life. A few years in Dubai were followed by many more years in Singapore.

Although it was exciting for her, she knew at a deep level that she was not honoring her soul contract.

And so the time came for us to intervene and introduce ourselves. We had been waiting patiently for many years for this moment to arrive.

Hello Erika

It was a normal Tuesday afternoon in Singapore when she arrived at the Polo Club. The sun was high in the sky and the trees were desperately praying for an afternoon monsoon to cool them down while they held the city in their arms. The streets were buzzing with cars, crowds of people and many blue taxis, all forming part of the clockwork of a bustling city. The air smelled of fried fish and everybody was on a mission, trying to accomplish something.

She was introduced to the polo trainers, all of whom came from Pakistan. Then she walked up and greeted all the animals. She was short with medium-length brown hair, well-dressed and immaculately groomed like all the Club members were. Her husband followed slightly behind.

She paused for a moment as she walked past my stable.

"What is her name?" she asked the groom.

"Erika," he replied.

"Isn't she beautiful?" she said, admiring my powerful, well-defined, muscular body.

She looked deeply into my soft, brown eyes and I smelled her perfume. For a split second our souls connected, and I knew in that instant that I had been waiting many years for this moment.

I could sense the fatigue in her physical body from the stress of keeping it all together – settling into a new job in a new country, with a different language and culture and with no support. I allowed her to rest against my chest while I sniffed the fragrance of her shampoo. I was thinking what an extraordinary journey it must have been for a farm girl from Africa, married to a Chinese man and ending up in Singapore.

She and her husband came back to the Club every weekend to ride. She always arrived with so much joy and excitement, and I could sense that this was her sanctuary. Here with me and all the other horses, she could be herself. Here she felt loved, accepted and ultimately free from the stress and responsibility of her daily life. Here she could breathe again, and here a very special bond started to develop, which was clearly not of this world.

As she spent more and more time with me, I got to know her better and the rest of her story unfolded.

She told me that her husband Jeff had had a heart attack the very day that they were supposed to leave Dubai for Singapore. He was on horseback when he had the attack, and the horse literally saved his life! He sensed that there was something wrong with his rider, so he walked slowly back to the stables while the rest of the group carried on riding. As if this event was not carefully designed and synchronized by us ...

She arrived in Singapore, vulnerable and all on her own, while her husband was recovering in a Dubai hospital. She had only one week to find a home for them and to deal with all the logistical arrangements before Jeff arrived. Her precious dogs would also be released from quarantine the following week.

Her two dogs, Malik and Tamara, had both been rescued from the desert in Dubai, and she was so grateful that she was able to take them with her to Singapore. They brought a piece of the desert with them.

While settling in and dealing with all the stressors of a global relocation, she also had to maintain a very demanding career, which sadly no longer inspired her soul. There was no mercy: a girl had to do what a girl had to do! So she worked the long, meaningless hours required of her.

When she got off the plane in Singapore to start her new life, a Johnny Walker advertisement in the airport caught her eye. This inspired her motto: 'Keep on Walking' regardless of how heavy her heart felt at that time.

ERIKA

After a couple of weeks, life started to flow into a new routine – a routine characterized by extreme busyness: grueling days, long working hours, endless meetings with no end in sight, extensive overseas travels, and most exhausting, late-night conference calls with her colleagues in America.

She was so tired of all the busyness and it was starting to show, but she couldn't slow down. This fast-paced life was all she had known her whole life. Everyone else was doing it, so it felt like the norm.

She felt trapped like a mouse on a treadmill: the faster she ran, the more tired she became, and the less inspired she felt.

At the same time, she started developing friendships that helped her cope with the demands of her daily existence. These friendships paved the way for what was to come, even though she had no idea what challenges life had in store for her; how she would need to hang on to the motto 'Keep on Walking'.

Lovely dinner parties characterized her social life. The smell of mouth-watering food and good com-

pany are pleasures that she treasures, even today, as her fondest memories of living in Singapore. Her friends came from all walks of life, brought together by their desire to stay fit and live healthily.

She came to the Club every weekend and even some evenings. Here she found her sanity and joy. We were like fountains, drinking from each other's streams.

ERIKA

❦

YOLANDA

A NORMAL SUNDAY MORNING

I was introduced to yoga while living in Singapore and felt drawn to the many benefits that this ancient practice had to offer.

My Sunday mornings were normally spent with Erika at the Club, followed by yoga lessons, then lunch with my husband, Jeff. Oh, the many restaurants to choose from and the variety of good food to explore! These were definite highlights of my weekends – the smells, the textures, the different tastes and the constant debate about which cuisine tasted better.

It was after one of those yoga sessions that I returned home and developed a major headache, followed by double vision. Suddenly, I could see two Maliks and two Tamaras. I went to lie down and after a short while it went away, so life carried on at its normal busy pace.

It was during a routine medical checkup, before yet another business trip the following week, that I told my doctor of the headache and the double vision. He was immediately alarmed and suggested that I go for a brain scan. I thought he was being too conservative. Both my husband and I dismissed the idea, believing that everything was fine.

There are certain things in life that you can hide away from for only a while before they catch up with you. I soon discovered that no matter how hard I tried, I could not ignore the doctor's suggestion any longer. It was a constant nagging thought, always lingering in the background.

One Friday afternoon I called the doctor and told him that I was ready to go for the scan, and it was booked for the following day.

ERIKA

༺❀༻

When she arrived at the Club the following afternoon, I could sense that something was different. There was a fear in her eyes that I had never seen before. She looked vulnerable and helpless. I gently nudged her against her shoulder, as if to say, "What's the matter?"

Words are not always necessary, and I sensed while she was leaning against me that she was embarking on the greatest challenge of her life, and that her human spirit would be tested like never before. I also knew that I would be there for her, every step of the way, as it was written in our contract. She told me that she went for a brain scan that morning and was awaiting the results.

༺❀༻

❧

THE OPERATION

It was 10 o'clock on a Monday morning when I received a phone call from the doctor. "They have discovered something on your brain and the brain surgeon will see you at twelve today!"

I waited anxiously for the appointment with the brain surgeon. I had never met a brain surgeon before in my life. What do they look like? What type of food do they eat?

A pair of emotionless eyes stared back at me, "You have a pineal gland tumor." His voice faded away as I tried to process the information. What is a brain tumor? Is it something that happens to sick people? How can this be happening to me?

He went on to explain that the pineal gland is situated in the middle of the brain and because of its location in the brain, it would be too risky to operate. It was causing a blockage of fluid in my brain, hence the double vision.

A pineal gland tumor is normally found in children, so it was very rare in a 43-year-old woman. The pineal gland is associated with the spiritual third eye. There was a lot to process. There was a lot going on.

I had lived a very simple life – no meat, no alcohol, no cigarettes, and I regarded myself a health fanatic with a regular daily exercise routine. This should not happen to me. It was as if I was having a horrible dream in which I was drowning. In the background, I could hear Jeff, my husband, and the doctor having a conversation about a brain operation and the different types of radiation treatments that were available to me. It was a clinical, matter-of-fact discussion, as if I was not even in the room.

When I managed to catch my breath, I heard myself asking the question, "How long do I have to live?"

"You have a long life ahead of you!"

I felt as though a lifeboat had just rescued me and that a second chance had been given to me, because I knew until then, I had only been living my life. I had not been true to my soul's purpose.

While we were talking about the brain operation and where they would put the shunt to drain the excess fluid, I tried to assess the doctor. I tried to connect to the soul behind the emotionless eyes. I looked at his hands. They were thin and long, the type of hands I always thought brain surgeons should have. I heard myself say, "You look too young to be a brain surgeon!"

"I am 41 years old," he said.

I am two years older, and what have I done wrong to manifest this thing in my brain? I have been on this planet for 43 years – what have I achieved? Have I used my time wisely? Have I left a legacy? All these questions were at the back of my mind as I was forced back to reality; to all the tests that needed to be done before the operation.

I woke on Wednesday, 21 January, 2007, with the alarm going off announcing the beginning of yet another day. The air that I breathed was telling me that this was not going to be a normal Wednesday.

As I did my morning meditation, I realized that today was the day the Divine was going to carry me in His arms. Some things in life are not meant to be dealt with alone.

I tried to joke with the nurses as they prepared me for brain surgery. It was as if my sense of denial was giving me more strength.

The brain surgeon was going to put a shunt in my brain to drain the excess fluid caused by the blockage formed by the brain tumor.

My sister Louise and her husband Lyall had flown in from South Africa to be with me. When she walked into the room, I felt as if I could face the world again. The power of love and family support are contracts made long before we enter the Physical Plane.

We are all spiritual beings experiencing a physical reality on this planet, and the people closest to us are those with whom we have special contracts to learn certain important lessons – like Erika who was patiently waiting at the stables as I underwent one of the most challenging experiences of my life.

The nurse entered the ward: "The operation staff is here, Mrs. Sing." I looked at my husband, and my sister and her husband, and I could feel fear gripping my body. I did not want to leave them, but some things are destined and beyond our control.

I waited on the operating table for the doctor to arrive. Everything was clean and sterile; the air was cold and had a smell of clinical anticipation about it. As the operating staff ran around making last-minute preparations, I wondered about the paths we had all travelled to meet there that morning. Who were these strangers whose eyes stared at me over their surgical masks? What were their dreams, fears and hopes, and what did they think of me lying here in a foreign country, only 43 and diagnosed with a brain tumor?

The doctor arrived. "How are you?" he asked. I looked deeply into his brown eyes. He looked different from the day before and I could sense his consternation. It was as if many lifetimes had passed between us. Why have I drawn you into my life to do this operation? What is the story that we can't remember? I only met you two days ago and now I am putting my brain in your hands. There must be a bigger picture! A deeper meaning! We will only understand when we re-evaluate our lives in the presence of the Divine one day!

Within a few minutes, I was pulled into a world of no feelings. I was floating without worries. I could get used to this. Where do our souls travel to when we are under anesthetic? Do we go to heaven to get extra support or do we just float above the clouds?

"Yolanda, you are doing very well." I heard the voice of the anesthesiologist.

"Is everything okay?" I asked.

"You are doing very well," replied the doctor.

"Thank you, God!"

After a day in hospital, I was discharged, but it was only the beginning of a very long journey. I was relieved that the operation went well but extremely frightened by the radiation and chemo-therapy that lay ahead. What a life-changing journey it proved to be!

❧

꧁ꕥ꧂

She returned to the Club a couple of days later. By then her hair was cut short and she had her family with her. She looked pale and weak. She told me that she had been diagnosed with a brain tumor and had already had brain surgery, and that radiation treatment would start the following week. She said it all as a matter of fact, but I could see the devastation in her eyes. All of them were dealing with something so much bigger than anything they had dealt with before and I knew in that moment that life was showing them all what truly mattered.

꧁ꕥ꧂

RADIATION

It was a cold Saturday morning when I walked into the radiation centre. I felt scared and intimidated by the newness of the situation.

A nurse who had a lovely smile on her face and softness in her eyes met me. I immediately liked her.

She took me to the preparation room, where they prepared the mask that would be fitted on my head. The mask was made of blue plastic, very similar to a Halloween mask! It would be used to channel the radiation beams, so it was extremely important that it fitted my head precisely.

I was scheduled to receive 25 radiation sessions, lasting between eight and ten minutes per session.

During my first radiation treatment, the room was full of nurses. I was lying on my stomach, with the mask tightly fitted on my head. It was very uncomfortable because I couldn't move and I had no control over the situation. It reminded me of prisoners being executed on an electric chair.

The air was cold and clinical. The nurses worked with precision and it was clear that they had all been very well trained. A radiation room is no place for errors. The radiation machine looked daunting and intimidating. It was a huge machine with energy of its own. I still remember the background music that was playing in the room – 'Country roads, take me home' by John Denver. The Universe surely has a sense of humor!

The big door closed behind the doctor and the nurses, leaving me on my own with the radiation machine for my first treatment. The atmosphere was electrifying. How did I get here, I wondered? Here I was in a foreign country, lying with my head in a mask, tied to a table in front of a big radiation machine. Again all the questions: What did I do wrong? Did the Divine forget about me? Am I cursed?

As the radiation machine started the session, I decided to change my thoughts. I quietly affirmed, "I thank the Universe for my complete health." So that became my daily affirmation, through all the radiation sessions.

It was a sad day when I had to take my leave of the radiation machine. I had realized that it had actually become my friend and that I had been looking forward to our daily meetings. But all good things must come to an end. I asked each staff member to sign my mask and write a little note for me to always remember the special time that they shared with me.

The hospital staff at both the Radiation and On-cology centers are all angels disguised as human beings. It takes a special soul to work with this

YOLANDA

type of intensity every day. I especially admire those who have not lost their kindness and caring attitudes, expressed by friendly smiles or a gentle hand on your shoulder – especially when the road ahead looks dark and frightening.

❧

Don't touch the spine

She was very nervous before her first radiation session. She was truly relieved when she visited me afterwards, realising that it is a quick and relatively painless exercise. Uncomfortable yes, because they put her head into a very tight clamp to keep it completely still, but definitely not painful.

She explained how she looked at the big radiation machine before her first treatment and acknowledged it for the healing energy that it would pour into her brain. She recalled the nervousness of the nursing sisters and the doctor because it was her first treatment and there was no room for error.

The radiation days were happy days for me because she came to visit me every afternoon. She was not allowed to ride during this time. I knew that it would be a couple of months before she would be able to ride again. Some things I just knew.

Members of the Club commented on her new hairstyle. When she told them that she had been diagnosed with a brain tumor and was undergoing radiation treatment, I could see how they literally stepped away from her. They could not deal with their own vulnerability and mortality in the face of her illness. I could sense her pain and feelings of utter rejection.

During this time, she came to the Club many afternoons, sitting quietly in my stable with her books. She was like a sponge, absorbing all that was written about alternative healing practices and the body's ability to heal itself. She told me how Gaya, her spiritual coach and mentor, helped her to apply many of these principles. I smiled quietly; I knew that Gaya was working with us, working together to bring about a major transformation. She was meant for bigger things.

I really enjoyed the radiation days as it had little or no impact on my body.

It was also a time for spiritual healing and cleansing – I had time to reflect on my life thus far. The journey from *doing* to *being* is scary as we are faced with some uncomfortable truths.

It was also during this time that the Universe brought Gaya into my life. She was a spiritual coach I had met a couple of months before. There was an immediate connection between us and I knew instinctively that Gaya had been sent to provide additional spiritual support during this trying time.

I felt stuck and trapped in a corporate career that no longer inspired me. I knew that I was destined for greater things, but did not know what they were or how to get there. Strange how feeling trapped in a transactional corporate job can be a substitute for living an inspired life.

I battled to understand why I manifested a brain tumor in my pineal gland, the gland that is regarded as the spiritual third eye. The doctors explained to me that this kind of tumor is mostly found in children, seldom in a mature woman in her early forties.

During this time *The Secret* by Rhoda Byrne was published and everybody was talking about our ability to manifest our own futures. Gaya played a pivotal role by guiding and coaching me on the Laws of the Universe that support the manifestation process.

What better place or time to start applying these laws! It was time to start healing my brain tumor – the one in the pineal gland right in the middle of my brain, apparently inoperable.

The Universe did not play around with this one. This was a major-league test with no room for error.

I knew that there were two processes occurring at the same time. Firstly, there was the clinical, medical process of the brain operation in conjunction with the radiation. Secondly, there was a spiritual energy process, which was far more important and challenging.

I studied every word in *The Secret*, and read every book I could find on healing from a spiritual perspective. I was stricken by fear of my own mortality. Was I preparing myself for death? And why are we so afraid of dying?

I knew intuitively that my healing would come first from deep meditation, prayer, breathing and healthy eating, rather than the medical process. Although I knew that the spirit commands, the mind obeys and the body depends, it was time to put it into practice and to align all parts of myself in order to work towards radiant health.

It was during this time of searching for the right answers that I learned the importance of doctors not projecting their own fears of death onto their patients or to view death as a failure on their part.

As the radiation treatments had little physical effect on me, I felt and looked very healthy. Incorporating juice from raw foods contributed to a radiant glow on my skin.

The only times I felt sick were when I had a doctor's appointment, during which they discussed the seriousness of the situation. On a spiritual level, I believed I was already cured and found it extremely frustrating that the scans did not reflect my beliefs.

The radiologist was concerned that the tumor might have spread down my spine, and the possibility of doing radiation treatments in that area was also mentioned. He had wanted to scan my spine at the beginning of the brain radiation treatments to accurately measure should they later on decide to continue with radiation directed onto my spine. Very reluctantly, I agreed to this.

The strangest thing happened as I was lying on the table, waiting for the X-ray to be taken. The X-ray machine broke down, something that hardly ever happens, especially not in a first-world country like Singapore! I stood up with a smile on my face and told the sister that this was a clear sign that no work would be done on my spine. And so it was!

I could do my own scans and did not need a machine to tell me what was wrong with me. It was very liberating to discover and trust this internal wisdom.

❧❧❧

❦

The most stressful days for all of us were the MRI days, and there were many of them! As the doctors knew, it was too dangerous to do a biopsy of the tumor because it was situated so deeply in the brain. So all diagnoses were based on the results of MRI scans. I noticed how she became quieter and more fragile as the days drew near. Luckily for all of us, the results were available immediately, so after an MRI morning I waited with anticipation for her.

I was always so happy when I saw her arrive with a big smile on her face and I knew that it was good news. The only way that I could celebrate with her was just to stand next to her and nuzzle my nose in her chest. My way of saying: "Well done, you go for it, girl!"

The curved ball

We had all been so excited and celebrated the results of the brain scans, accepting them with joy and gratitude. How devastating it was for all of us who had travelled the journey with her when life threw her an unexpected curve ball!

Chinese New Year is a big celebration over three to four public holidays. Everything comes to a halt as the Chinese celebrate the birth of a new year. She was scheduled for her last MRI on the Thursday before the beginning of Chinese New Year. We were all looking forward, eager to return to a normal life.

She did not return to the stables for some time after her last scan. I knew that something was wrong and then, at last, she came! I was so relieved, hiding my face, scared that she would see the happiness in my eyes.

ERIKA

This time she looked extremely fragile and she could not hold back the tears. A blood vessel had burst in her eye, a sign of the many tears that had already been shed. I let her bury her face in my neck. While she sobbed softly, she told me that she was scheduled for intensive chemotherapy treatment. She did not know where she was going to get the strength from to handle this ordeal. It had never been part of the doctor's original treatment plan.

❧

On Friday afternoons, I was usually in a business class lounge on my way back from an overseas business trip, but this Friday I was walking into an oncologist's consulting room.

My first reaction was to think that I did not belong here, and that I was too smart to be sick. I was mesmerized by the real world − it was unfolding right in front of my eyes. It was a far cry from the corporate boardrooms where egos dominated a game. This was life in its most intense and raw form.

Soon the realisation set in that this was part of my journey and that there was a mountain to be climbed!

ERIKA

❧

Slowly but surely she started preparing for the first series of chemotherapy treatments. I noticed that her hair had been cut even shorter and she was becoming more withdrawn as the big day approached.

Martie, one of her friends from South Africa, decided to come and stay with them for a couple of weeks, and she was looking forward to the visit and moral support.

She was still very strong during the first sessions of chemotherapy, and she and Martie visited me often. I saw that her hair was becoming noticeably thinner and that she appeared more fragile and vulnerable.

On the days when she was feeling fine, she loved to visit, challenging all of us to get used to her without any hair.

The cumulative effect of the chemotherapy made her too weak to visit me often. I saw less and less of her. It did not bother me much as I knew that we were one, and that I was there with her in spirit, every step of the way.

ERIKA

჻჻჻

THE CALL

A nother Monday morning in Singapore and the phones were ringing incessantly. But I found myself not in my office but in the Oncology Unit. Nurses dressed in white were getting ready for another week of healing. I had been asked to come in very early as it was my first day of chemotherapy treatment and measurements had to be taken.

The alarm had gone off at the usual time and I'd started my day as I always did. It was raining as I sat outside on my patio, surrendering the day to the Divine and asking for His special Angels to be with me on this day.

The previous evening I had wondered what to pack in my bag to take with me to the Oncology Clinic – maybe something to read and some water to drink. But deep inside, I knew I needed much more than water and books. I was signing up for the biggest battle of my life. So what do you take with you to the battlefield? I decided on hope, faith, a positive attitude and an inner knowing, allowing the Divine within to lead the way.

Mornings are extremely busy at the Oncology Center. The gray chairs wait patiently for their occupants to arrive. Nurses rush around, preparing each patient's chemotherapy for the day. The air smells of disinfectant. Everything gets checked. Everything gets double-checked. Perfection must be ensured. There must be no doubt that all systems work.

The nurse's face was emotionless as she prepared the drip.

"What is your name?" I asked.

As she answered, I wondered how many patients she had treated who had won the battle and how many had moved on to the Other Side. I waited in anticipation as she opened the drip, and as the first drop of chemotherapy entered my body, I affirmed, "Welcome to my body and let's fight this battle together."

The expressions on the faces of the other patients were mixed. Everybody was searching for the strength within as we all fought the same battle. I suppose it was not just the fight against cancer but also the fight against our own mortality. In some eyes I saw hope, and in others an emptiness that made my stomach turn.

I looked at all the people around me and wondered how they all got here. I stood out like a sore thumb — I was not only the youngest patient; I was also the only patient of Western origin.

How do you sign up for the battle against cancer? Is it Karma, unhealthy lifestyle, genes, or a combination of these factors? Or is it simply that the Divine has favorites and loves others more? All these questions had been haunting me for the last couple of weeks. I had always lived my life very close to the Divine. I started every morning with a five o'clock meditation, and tried consciously not to hurt other people. Was this the reward for doing the right thing? I had searched for God in the eyes of other people, the voices and words of hope of others. But where are you God when we need you the most? What is the purpose of suffering? For that matter, what is the purpose of life?

All these questions whirled in my mind as I watched the other cancer patients walk past me with drips in their hands and emptiness in their eyes.

The nurse came to check my drip. As I stared at her face, I felt as if a permanent white light was protecting her from having any emotional contact with me. It was as if they had been trained to do their job meticulously and not to get involved with each patient's story. Was that because they had been hurt before by getting too attached and then having to say goodbye? Who knows the stories we all have to tell?

Losing my hair

YOLANDA

Nothing could have prepared me for the emotional impact the loss of my hair would have on me. Standing in the shower with my hair streaming down my face was such a profound experience. Part of me wanted to hang on to it because it symbolized life to me, a life that I knew was not working. Yet another part of me wanted to hang on to it because, at the time, it was the only life that I knew. I was in my comfort zone and change was scary.

Typical of my controlling personality, I was well prepared for this event. I had bought a wig a month in advance and had also got my hairdresser to style it for me. My husband, who is very fashion conscious, had also bought me a variety of caps. It was important for him that I looked good, despite the chemotherapy.

How special it was when he said, "You have the features to pull it off and I love you with or without your hair."

Those words will always stay with me.

And yet, when it came to wearing the wig or the caps, something deep inside me resented it. I wanted to be self-assured, regardless of my looks. I wanted to carry the signs of this disease with pride because I knew therein lay my victory. I did not want to be a victim as that energy no longer served me.

You see, for my whole life I had always hidden behind something – hairstyles, well-groomed personal appearance, perfectly manicured nails, tailored suits, Gucci shoes and Louis Vuitton handbags. It was as though I needed these things as crutches to lean on in order for people to accept me as someone who had made it. Made what? By whose standards? And at what price?

This time a different force was motivating me. I wanted to stand naked in front of the mirror and reveal my true self. I wanted to accept my graying hair and not hide behind six-weekly color treatment shampoos. I wanted to accept my droopy boobs and the cellulite on my legs.

I wanted to honor my body with all its short-comings, because going through the radiation and chemo treatments I revealed how strong I really was.

The time had come to truly stand in my brilliance and to stop making excuses. The time had come for true self-acceptance and to stop swimming upstream.

Without knowing it at the time, I was giving birth to a new me. I wanted to start living without fear and to embrace my unique voice to this world. It was time to declare who I really am, and to stop fearing it.

And yet, when people stared at me in shopping centers, I wondered whether I would be strong enough to pull it off. What did they think when they looked at me? Were they thinking that I was preparing for my own death? Was I perhaps preparing for my own death?

Facing our mortality is one of the scariest processes, but it is essential to a deep understanding of true surrender and authenticity.

Thanks to my psychology background, I knew that they were only projecting their own fears onto me, but that did not make me feel any better. I could sense the sorrow in their eyes as they stared at me. Simple questions − like my yoga teacher putting his arm around me and asking how I felt, or the groom at the stables asking why I had cut my hair so short − had become extremely difficult to answer.

I have never encouraged people to feel sorry for me. Regardless of my circumstances, I always appeared self-assured and in control. So when people started to stare at me with my perceived sorrow in their eyes, I resented every moment of it.

However, these experiences were teaching me the important lesson of accepting myself as a unique and unconventional human being. Until then, I had always needed to be liked by others, and for the first time my brain tumor taught me the important lesson of true authenticity: to realize that the people who love you do not care about your hairstyle and that acceptance means not hiding behind anything, not even a hairstyle.

This was a profound, life-changing lesson for me. I wondered how else I would have learnt the lesson of truly accepting my uniqueness if it had not been for my chemotherapy experience.

I realized that the Universe always knows best.

Controlling the outcome

One of the burdens that I had been carrying with me from an early age was the need to always be in control. It started when I learnt that you need to perform in order to be showered with love and acceptance. I had just never realized how entrenched this belief was and how deeply this need had become part my being. It was like a cancer cell that had grown and overtaken my psyche.

It was a Tuesday morning, on 10 April, when I walked into the oncologist's rooms. I was not scheduled to see him until early the following week. This appointment was at my request.

I walked in with self-confidence and I asked if we could start the second round of chemotherapy a week earlier because I felt ready and strong enough.

My chemo treatments were divided into three cycles of three weeks each. In the first week you receive 15 hours of chemo treatment; in the second week you feel sick and extremely exhausted; and in the third week the body rebuilds itself. It was during the beginning of the third week that I felt so strong and confident that I believed that I could start the chemo treatment during that week.

The oncologist looked at me with amusement and shock. He could not believe his ears. "We cannot start the treatment earlier," he said. "You have no idea of all the processes that are currently happening in your body. It is not about how you feel. The answer is No. Good-bye."

I walked out of his office with my tail between my legs. I had been looking for recognition and instead I was slapped on my wrist.

What motivated me to do this? It was only the next day, when I reflected in a session with my counselor, that the real learning happened.

What motivated me were impatience and an internal assumption that I am not normal. By completing the treatment earlier, I thought that I would have my life back.

The lesson was much deeper than that. For my whole life, I had been striving for normality and it took a brain tumor to make me realize that I am unique, different and unconventional.

My family expected me to stay within my tribe, marrying a husband from my own culture, one who would be able to take care of my financial needs. They expected me to live in South Africa, have children and lead a traditional life. I did not do any of that.

Because my mother died when I was three months old, I have always known intuitively that my journey was not going to be normal. And even though I knew it, my shadow side was pulling me back to the idea that other people would accept me only if my life was normal.

It was a breakthrough to realize that I had to change my internal assumption because my life would never be normal. I was born to run wild and embrace my own uniqueness. Normality would not bring out the best in me because my uniqueness is one of the building blocks of my creativity.

So although I walked out of the oncologist's rooms with my tail between my legs, I am ever grateful for the profound insight that was hidden behind the situation.

Living in the moment and trusting that the Universe would give me the means to release the need to control the outcome. This would be a challenging journey, but one that I had already embarked on.

Where are you on your journey of accepting your own uniqueness? Or are you also trying to conform to society's standards of what your life should be? It is only by breaking away from society's expectations and by embracing our uniqueness that we will all experience true liberation.

The storm before the calm

My mother came to visit me during my last chemotherapy cycle, because she had heard that the last cycle is the most demanding of all. I did not really pay much attention to this prediction, as I believed that it would become easier since the body would already be used to the treatment. How ignorant and naïve can one be?

I can honestly say that last chemotherapy cycle was the worst. No words can describe the feeling of exhaustion and weakness I experienced. I did not even have the energy to get out of bed. Just getting out of bed and brushing my teeth were huge accomplishments.

The extreme humidity and heat in Singapore were sucking the last bit of energy from my body. In addition, our neighbours were renovating their home so I was subjected to constant noise of drilling and banging on the walls. It is a time that is forever imprinted on my mind.

I had always been very proud of my body; fit enough to keep up with all the younger students at a power yoga class. All of a sudden, it became a stranger to me. It felt as if I were living in someone else's body. What had happened to all the power and vitality that was once there?

The emotional pressure in our house reflected the outside temperatures. It was extremely challenging for my mother and husband to see me suffering so much. They felt so helpless as there was nothing they could do for me. For days on end, they just sat next to my bed. I could sense the tension between them, as if they wanted to blame each other for my discomfort.

One afternoon I went to the kitchen to fetch some water. I was so weak and exhausted that I passed out on the floor. I had always been the strong and successful one, and here I was, lying on the kitchen floor. Life knew that the only way to deal with my ego was to literally bring me to my knees.

During those days I struggled constantly with the Divine. I wanted Him to take this burden away from me. I started to believe that He was punishing me for something I had done in the past. At one stage, I was not praying to live; rather, I was asking to be taken away very gently to the Other Side. But the Divine knew that I had to stay a little longer in the valley of the shadow of the death. My lesson was not over yet.

I woke up on a bright Wednesday morning, after yet another difficult night, and made a conscious decision that it was going to be a good day. I could no longer stand the feeling of being sick, depressed, scared and weak. I told my family about my positive decision and that fateful Wednesday became the turning point in my recovery.

It was as if the Divine wanted me to take the first step before He held me in His arms. I knew that I was still very weak and recovery would take some time, but on that Wednesday morning I signed up to live, to take on life and all the challenges that were still ahead of me.

The last chemo

I had lived and dreamt about the last day of chemotherapy treatment for months, and finally it arrived. Both my mother and my husband were in good spirits as we got ready to go to the clinic.

I asked my friend to bring some gifts from South Africa and Jeff had bought a chocolate cake to celebrate the last day of chemotherapy. My appreciation was sincere as they had all been so kind to me.

My excitement was contagious and they all shared in my joy.

I received a little handmade card from the oncologist and the staff.

As I waited for the last chemo drip to finish, I could not help but notice the despair in the patients all around me. My chemo treatment had a beginning and an end date, but many patients are on chemo treatment until the last days of their lives. I was very sensitive to that and did not want to be disrespectful of their situation.

I had asked the oncologist a few days before if we could remove the line from my shoulder. A line is a semi-permanent drip that they put in your shoulder instead of in your hand to administer the chemo. The oncologist did not want to damage my pretty hands! He said that we could remove the line after my last chemo treatment.

I felt absolute joy when the nurse removed the line! The freedom to have a bath without asking someone to wrap me up or go to yoga class without people staring at the drip in my shoulder! I felt normal again and I was so very grateful to have reached this important milestone.

The removal of the line also symbolized hope to me. At that time, there was no guarantee that the chemo had worked or that I would not require more treatments. But by removing the line, I believed in the doctor and his knowledge, believing that no further treatments would be required. For the next six weeks I clung to that hope. My follow-up scan was already arranged and diarized.

Strangely, I also had mixed feelings about leaving the Oncology Center.

The times spent there were the most intense of my life and, in a way, the brain tumor had become my daily companion. Going to the Center had given me a purpose in life, a daily routine that somewhat resembled normal. The staff had come to know a very authentic Yolanda, a person very different from the persona that I projected at work.

Who am I and who have I become? Little did I know how important these questions would become in the days ahead!

❦

SAYING GOODBYE

It was time for my mother to return to South Africa. Saying goodbye to her was not an easy task. Part of me yearned to be a child again, carefree and someone else's responsibility. We could both feel the pressure as the day of her departure drew nearer. It was as if we had an unspoken agreement that we would be strong for each other. Thinking back, I realized that it was not the first time that we had had to do this.

We have had many goodbyes in our lives. The first day she took me to enroll at primary school: I had to stay in the school hostel – at the tender age of six because our farm was too far away from town. Then to the university in Bloemfontein, a five-hour drive away from home, and finally, to my first job in Cape Town. Cape Town is known as the Mother City, but it surely sucks when you are all alone. We had many memories of saying goodbye and crying on each other's shoulders. But knowing how to say goodbye did not make it any less painful.

The morning after her departure I entered her bedroom. Her perfume still hung in the air and her presence was all around me. I was overcome by unbearable feelings of emptiness and sadness.

I went outside to the patio where my mom and my friend had spent many hours with me. Suddenly, there was only silence and my own company. Even the neighbor's renovations had come to an end. It was as if the whole chemo experience had been surreal, as if it had never happened. In the bathroom I stared into the mirror, looking at my bloated cheeks and bald head, the stark reminders of the months gone by. No, I had not been dreaming.

Why is life so complicated? Why can't we just be happy? Why can't things work out perfectly all the time? Why must people go through chemo experiences? Why are some people blessed and others not?

All these questions and no answers — little did I know that life was teaching me one of the most profound lessons of all — the art of manifesting, and co-creating, with the Divine, the life that I was intended to live.

$$\mathcal{C}\text{\tiny{\textbf{\%}}}\mathcal{O}$$

EVERYDAY BEAUTY

Jeff and I started preparing for a short holiday to Bali. We both desperately needed to get away from our immediate environment. The oncologist felt that we were planning the holiday too soon after the chemo, but we went ahead anyway.

My first swim in the ocean was pure joy. I felt so alive as the water splashed against my body. It felt as if the ocean was washing away all the chemo from my veins and purifying and cleansing my aura. I had not felt so happy in years.

The long walks on the beach, traditional Bali massages and beautiful dinners were just what we needed to recover from our ordeal.

I started paying more attention to the small things in life. I started appreciating a sunset more, because I had learnt that we do not know what tomorrow will bring. I suppose I was learning to live in the moment.

I also did my first off-road bicycle ride in Bali. The owner of the villa where we stayed was a keen off-road mountain biker. He offered to take us on an off-road ride to see the rice fields. He warned us that the ride would be strenuous, but little did I know how strenuous, yet beautiful, it would be.

We did an 18-kilometer ride over treacherous terrain in humid heat. When I got off the bike, I felt like a different person – stronger and alive. I had proved to myself that I could believe in my body again. Our guide did not treat me like a sick person, although the signs of the recent chemotherapy treatment were written all over me. It was my first baby step on the journey of rebuilding my body and believing in myself again.

D-day or a clear day

Before I knew it, it was time for my brain to be scanned again. The day started like any other, but again I could feel that it was going to be totally different.

The scan was scheduled for 8.30 am and the appointment with the oncologist for 1.30 pm. By now, I was used to the MRI machine and the narrow tunnel no longer intimidated me.

While they were doing the scan, I again affirmed my thanks to the Universe for my complete and utter health.

As always, my husband was there with me, patiently waiting. Only looking back on those hours of waiting does one realize that quietly sitting on the sideline has its own implications.

We went back home, both trying very hard to be strong for one another. I knew that all my family and friends were waiting in anticipation for my phone call — a phone call that would drastically change the direction of my life. Unbeknown to me, many of my friends, their friends and their families had started a prayer group all over the world, praying for this exact moment when the Divine would shower me with His love and grace.

In the midst of all the pressure, I had a sense of calm. Was I learning to accept my own mortality and the ultimate realisation that we are all spiritual beings having a human experience, and that ultimately we will all return home?

I had to collect my own test results and take them to the oncologist's rooms. I was too scared to look at the results myself. I was carrying the test results that would change my future, my life, and yet I did not have the courage to open the envelope. With a feeling of utter relief I handed them over to the receptionist.

The doctor's rooms were particularly busy that afternoon. It was strange to be back in that environment. I felt as if I no longer belonged there. Yet from the look on the other patients' faces, I could tell that they thought I was still part of the team. I still had no hair.

We had to wait two hours before the oncologist could see us. Those two hours felt like two days. The pressure of waiting was unbearable. I held onto my husband's hand and watched the other patients having chemo treatments.

As they left the chemo center, I felt so sorry for them as I knew what challenging and difficult days lay ahead of them. The expression of emptiness in their faces, the concern of their loved ones, and the efficiency of the nurses again touched me. It was like a production line with no place for error or human emotion.

"Mrs. Sing," I heard the receptionist call my name. I looked at my husband, took a deep breath, surrendered the moment to the Divine, and walked into his office.

The oncologist was in a good mood. For him I was just another patient, but for me, this was one of the most important moments in my life. As usual, he wanted to weigh me first. I was visibly shaking as I stood on the scale.

He looked at the test results and told me that there would always be a scar in my brain. I asked him whether I had cancer and he said, "No."

I asked him whether I should be regarded as a sick person and again he said, "No."

I closed my eyes and thanked the Divine for giving me a second chance. He continued his physical examination, gave me a medical report and asked me to come back in eight weeks' time for another blood test.

I looked at Jeff, unable to believe the good news. I immediately called my family, first my sister and then my mom. In the end, we were all in tears. I called my close friends and my spiritual coach, Gaya, all of whom were overjoyed.

The first thing I did when we got home was sit on the patio where I had spent so many hours. I closed my eyes and thanked the Universe for restoring my faith and for giving me my life back. With that came the responsibility of making the most of every moment.

We went out to celebrate that evening. I was grateful for Jeff who had been there with me every difficult step of the way.

We truly share a special bond with the life partners we choose to share this journey on Earth.

❧

The transition

We saluted her human spirit for enduring such a difficult life lesson with so much resilience.

We have watched the cleansing and detoxification process and we knew that the old was making way for the new.

It was time for her to claim her unique voice to the world.

༄

MY PASSION FOR HORSES

It was not until my mid-thirties that I discovered the beauty of horses. While working in Dubai, my good friends Julie and Emma introduced me to horses and horse riding.

I knew instantly that I was onto something that would have a profound impact on the rest of my life. It felt so good to be surrounded by these strong masculine animals, and I knew that something was shifting inside me. The more time I spent with them the more alive I felt.

The world of Equine Assisted Learning started to call me, as I had already attended a workshop in the United Kingdom the year before, and I knew that my unique calling to the world was to bridge the gap between the paddock and the boardroom.

Jeff and I also went to Spain to attend a course in horse whispering. During this holiday, something profound happened that changed my life forever.

I was asked to do very simple groundwork exercises with the horses. As I was struggling with one particular exercise, the horse looked straight into my eyes and in some inexplicable way, peeled off every layer of protection until only my core being remained.

Needless to say, it brought me to tears and it took me a long time to process what happened. After that holiday, I knew intuitively that horses would always be an important part of my life. They made me feel whole.

"The wind of heaven is that which blows between a horse's ears." (Arabian proverb)

Horses are such authentic animals. They cannot lie to you. They simply reflect your non-verbal behavior as they tune into your vibrational frequency. They are the best psychologists on Earth.

Dada was one of the mares at the Singapore Polo Club who had a reputation for being a difficult horse. She did not like humans and showed it by kicking or biting. I knew that fear caused her behaviour. She was scared because some human had treated her badly.

As I worked on building trust with Dada, I noticed a change in her. She was starting to chase the other horses away when they came to close to me. It was as if she was saying, "She belongs to me."

Dada developed a strong bond with me, and always looked at me with very sad eyes every time I left the Polo Club.

Shirley was a young Arab mare who came from Australia. She was used for the more experienced riders because she was extremely fast and her natural pace was a full gallop. Shirley had no stable manners and she did not like human touch. She communicated that by biting and kicking when you came near her. She only wanted to play polo.

To me, she represented my anger toward the Divine and the situation in which He had put me. I wished I could also kick and bite to get the situation to go away.

Over a period of weeks I noticed a change in Shirley's behaviour. She was starting to look forward to my visits and greeted me with softness in her eyes. Was it my own acceptance of the situation that she was reflecting to me?

Grandfather was a huge, strong, Arab stallion, also from Australia. I gave him the name of Grandfather because he was the proud patriarch of the yard.

Grandfather was an intimidating horse because he was big, strong, very fast, and he knew it. His strength attracted me the most. If I could fight this brain tumor with that kind of strength, I could also be a winner. Grandfather always looked forward to my stable visits. I discovered that he liked apples, and I never visited the stables without giving him his apple!

And then there was Erika, my very special polo pony. How could I describe her, a true soul mate who always knew and understood me? Words were never necessary because she understood and accepted me on the deepest level and without judgment. It was a very special bond and one that I will treasure for the rest of my life.

It was my dream of bridging the gap between the paddock and the boardroom that gave me hope and inspiration during my darkest hours. How can a person die with the song still in your heart?

The wig

I had mixed emotions at the thought of going back to work and re-entering society. I was happy to be busy and feel part of something again, but I was acutely aware of my baldness. It was easy to deal with strangers, but how would I approach my boss and my colleagues with no hair?

I felt uncomfortable wearing a wig – it felt as though I was undoing all the hard work I had done to reclaim my authenticity. Eventually, I decided to wear the wig to work, because I knew that it would be uncomfortable for my colleagues otherwise.

And so the journey with the wig began.

I soon realized that I no longer had the ability to connect with the triviality of corporate life. The small problems that consumed our days and the meaninglessness of corporate society no longer appealed to me.

I became more aware of how ungrateful people are and how they complain about trivial things. But how could I judge them when they had never been on the other side of the fence? It was just so much easier to be busy and spend long hours at the office and on the phone than to take responsibility and make the most of each day.

I also knew that they were mirroring part of my old self. I did not know how to deal with my newly found realizations. And yet this world had been part of my life for twenty years. Why had I never seen the wood for the trees? Had I also been so caught up in the ego and scarcity struggles at work that years had passed without my realizing it?

I felt like fish out of water.

I also went back to yoga classes. Some people were too scared to look me in the eye and some openly stared at my bald head. I held my head high and ignored all the stares. It was not long before they got used to my bald head, and I started feeling part of the class again. As my hair started growing back, people felt more comfortable to approach me. I could feel and see the admiration in their eyes, and their words of encouragement spurred me on to reclaim my fitness and suppleness.

It was good to feel alive again, and the Divine smiled.

The desired outcome

The oncologist asked me to go for a follow-up brain scan six weeks after my last chemo treatment.

My focus during those six weeks was on healthy eating and living as my body felt bloated from all the chemicals and steroids that had been pumped into it.

I knew intuitively that healthy living was important, but I needed much more than that. I continued my sessions with Gaya with the focus on restoring my faith in the Universe. She helped me to manifest the desired reality by helping me believe that I was already cured.

She asked me to create a vision board of pictures that represented my ideal life. I had to change the way I prayed. Instead of asking, I had to express my gratitude for having already been healed. I had to make a daily gratitude list and believe that I lived in a perfect and abundant world.

I had to continue my daily meditation sessions. The focus was on visualizing the desired outcome and truly connecting with my Source.

It was only while working with Gaya that I realized how much fear and darkness had crept into my existence. Frankly speaking, I was tired of leading a life filled with one human trauma after another. I knew that we come down to this Physical Plane to learn lessons that prepare us for a bigger task in the next dimension. However, I also realized that in the process I had lost my faith and trust in the Divine. I had actually started to believe that He was punishing me because I had done something terribly wrong.

After 43 years on this planet, not only was my physical body crying out for a different lifestyle, but so too my soul. When last had I wished for something good to happen to me? When last had I woken up in the morning and heard the birds singing? When last had I smelled freshly cut grass? When last had I really tasted my breakfast?

I could not ignore the wake-up call that the Universe was giving me. I had been so caught up in my corporate role, my Blackberry and the business-class lifestyle that I had forgotten what it was like to live without stress and fear. What had happened to my dreams?

It was a difficult journey to change my thinking. I had come to the conclusion that the biggest challenge in this human experience was to conquer our egos. When we have done that, we have obtained a first-class ticket to freedom and happiness. The ego was the little voice that told us that we were not good enough or smart enough, that we should be scared of life instead of embracing every minute of it.

I had to have a few difficult sessions with my ego, and I believe this will continue until the day I leave this planet. Just as I had to lose all my hair in order for the new me to emerge, so I had to cleanse my ego. I had to consciously tell it that the Divine is on my side. Life is too short to live a life filled with fear and stress.

Slowly I started to notice small changes emerge in my life. I felt happier and lighter. I laughed more and appreciated the small things in life. I no longer checked my Blackberry first thing in the morning; neither did I check it on the way to work. My focus was on the beauty of the day unfolding in front of me. I started to believe again that the Divine was on my side.

The most profound change was starting to think of my brain tumor as a special gift: an invitation to step out of my life and observe it from a distance so I could make the changes necessary for the second half of my life. I was truly blessed to have been chosen for this unique and special journey.

❧

❧

Leaving Gucci

All storms in the Universe come to an end, and so it was with this storm in her life. Soon it was time for her last MRI scan and I knew that as soon as she got the all-clear from the doctors, she would start riding again.

Miracles happen when we have enough trust and faith to believe that they can manifest in our lives. For the last couple of months, she had been exercising the muscles of trust and faith, and the Universe did not disappoint her.

Life soon returned to its normal routine: working, travelling and spending time with me over the weekends. Her hair grew back, although very curly and sometimes unrecognizable!

On the surface, it looked as if everything was back to normal, but I knew that deep inside she was no longer the person she was before the brain tumor. It had left a permanent scar on her psyche, a scar to remind her to follow her passion and be true to her soul's calling.

She realized that all the years in corporate life had numbed her. She had learnt not to express her emotions and had totally forgotten how to laugh. She had a yearning to feel alive again.

It was time to practise the spiritual lesson of surrender, which she had learned so well in the dark, chemotherapy days.

"Universe, you take it, because I can't deal with it," she told herself.

And again, the Universe did not disappoint her.

She came to the Club one day and told me with mixed emotions that she was moving back to South Africa to follow her soul's calling, and that she had decided to leave the corporate, jet-set lifestyle and her Gucci shoes behind in Singapore.

She was not sure how it would all work out, but she had trust, faith and a burning desire to make this happen, and sometimes that is all we all need.

And so the day approached for her to say good-bye to me. It was a build-up of emotions for both of us. I could see that she had been crying before she arrived at the stables. I wanted to make it easy for her, because I knew something that she still had to learn.

I gently nuzzled against her and licked her hands to express my gratitude for the all the love, caring and joy that she had brought into my life. We looked deeply into one another's eyes; she kissed me on the cheeks and quietly turned around and walked away.

More than perfect ... or perhaps not?

She once told me that the two most important decisions in support of changing her life and following her passion were to sleep more in her own bed than in a hotel bed and to speak to the people she liked after 6 p.m. in the evenings! And that is exactly what she did.

Her new lifestyle is a far cry from the jet-set, corporate lifestyle she left behind in Singapore. She has started her own company, CHLOE Consultants, offering global leadership development programmes that use horses to cross the bridge between the paddock and the boardroom.

She lives in a small homestead in the middle of the forest. Her stables are filled with horses, each with a special story to tell. Dogs, cats, geese and even a domesticated pig and tortoises fill her life with love and joy. She is surrounded by a beautiful garden. Growing organic vegetables is her aim, but the animals find them all too tempting. She is in love with the simplicity of it all. She is now following her passion in life. She is using horses to help people.

Life has certainly come full circle for her; she moved back to a small town, very close to the place where she was born.

Her immediate environment is a constant reminder of the journey she has travelled and of the place where it all started.

ERIKA

✿

ॐ

OUR TRIBE

Moving back home and reintegrating my expatriate global experience into a simple, country lifestyle were not without challenges. The isolation and the constant reminder of not belonging were overwhelming at times. It was during these times that the horses again surrounded and protected me.

Our family is our tribe and they are here to teach us some important lessons. I do believe that we choose them very carefully, long before our souls embark on this journey. They always mirror part of our own soul's healing and that is why it's sometimes so complicated and layered.

Some of us choose to take on the life lesson of no longer belonging to our tribe or fitting in. It is as though our tribe has rejected us, but actually we often do the rejecting.

Some of my friendships also did not stand the test of time. People share our lives for a reason and it is very challenging to let them go, especially when you intended the friendship to be life-long.

That was one of the many life lessons that I had to deal with when I moved back to South Africa.

My tribe was no longer my birthplace or country. Too much had happened for me to fit in. I had to deal with the bittersweet rejection of not fitting in, and had to learn to embrace the fact that I had become a child of the world.

I was no longer a farmer's daughter, and even though I tried to fit into the fabric of small-town society, I will always stand out proudly walking my path.

One cannot deny the people and the cultural experiences that have shaped our lives, and I have definitely taken some very rich, cultural experiences and memories back with me to Africa.

❧❧

❧

Finding Erika

*S*he loves sitting at her stables in the morning drinking a cup of tea, watching her dogs play, listening to the sound of the birds singing in the trees and the horses crunching their food; peaceful, calm, and without a care in the world. Her groom cares for the horses, busying himself in the yard while listening to his African music.*

It is time for reflection on her journey and for expressing gratitude for the beauty that surrounds her and for all the people who have travelled this journey with her.

She often thinks of Erika, the beloved polo pony she had to leave behind in Singapore during these meditation sessions.

It was during one of these sessions that she felt a gentle nudge, and when she looked up, there I was, as I have always been! She gently smiled and stroked my chin and we both knew that no time, place, or distance would ever break the bond between us, not in this or any other lifetime.

You see, it had all been written long before that I would guide her on this journey. I will always be part of the air that she breathes and she will be honored to be my voice in the paddock.

Appendix A.1

Gaya Wisdom and Clarity

The Art of Being

Don't try to force anything. Let life be a deep let-go. God opens millions of flowers every day without forcing their buds. Osho

It is a rainy Saturday afternoon and I am contemplating a week of being.

The realisation that we define ourselves by what we do, what we wear, and the type of people with whom we surround ourselves, has been haunting me this whole week.

The doing was removed from my life this week, and I have had to face myself without a job, conference calls, overseas travels and numerous e-mails and phone calls.

Who am I?

What have I become?

These are some of the questions that life is asking me to reflect on.

For my whole working life I had a love-hate relationship with busyness. The busier I was, the more in control I felt. Suddenly, there was nothing to control, only an opportunity to reflect and heal.

Who had I become?

The face in the mirror had become a stranger to me.

How do you reclaim parts of yourself you lost along the way? How do you get in touch with your inner child and the sparkling fire that the Divine has given all of us?

Sometimes it takes a brain tumor to force us to step back and take a deep look at what is really going on.

The most profound realization is that the work system continued without me. People I expected to call me showed no interest. How could I have thought that I played such an important role, when the system behaved otherwise?

It takes courage to explore the darkness within us. The lost pieces of our soul need a lot of nurturing and compassion to be woven back into a more centered and grounded sense of self – a self that will hopefully never allow the system to take our brilliance and uniqueness away again. Thank you, Source, for sending us life-transforming challenges, because the Sun always shines after the storm.

❧

❧

Appendix A.2

The Special People

It was a Sunday afternoon when I received an unexpected phone call from Sri Lanka.

"Hello, Madam, this is Dizna speaking. I have been praying so hard for you. How are you doing, Madam?"

Dizna, a Sri Lankan, was my domestic worker in Dubai and had since moved back to Sri Lanka to be with her family. She is a big, fat lady, with a voice that commands respect. You only need a Dizna around to sort out the workers around the house!

The call from Dizna really touched my heart. I knew that she was living on a small budget, and that an overseas call was a big expense for her, and yet she called to tell me that she was praying for me.

Who are the people whose lives we touch?

Sometimes we try so hard to influence the right people – bosses, potential friends, headhunters, and potential employers – and yet those people are hardly there for you when you walk in the valley of life.

Who are the people whose lives we touch? The Diznas in our lives are the people who really make a difference. They give from an unconditional place. They give because they really care and not because they can get something from you in return.

They are the people who make the journey on this Earth worthwhile. They put a smile on your face and surround your heart with a warm feeling of love, care and acceptance.

Thank you, Source, for knowing when to send us a Dizna.

Appendix A.3

The Power of Prayer

I have always believed in the power of prayer and thought I understood its meaning until my brain tumor came along.

I regard myself as a spiritual being with a strong connection with my Creator, although I do not follow any particular religion. I have always believed that I do not need systems or people between my Creator and myself. But sometimes we can all do with a little help.

One of my husband's friends offered to pray for me. At first she was hesitant to approach me as my religious beliefs were based on Eastern principles and she was not sure whether I would be open to a prayer group.

Little did she know that I pray and meditate every morning. Organized religions only divide people and I was so grateful to experience how our mutual connection to our Creator and a Higher Power were enough to bind us in prayer.

I started looking forward to our Tuesday prayer meetings. It was not long before another friend also joined the group.

For some strange reason, I became very emotional during these prayer groups. The sincerity of the prayers, the unconditional love of the group and most importantly, the presence of the Divine that I could feel so strongly, touched me at a very deep level.

When we connect with our Creator, there is no room for façades. Questions like 'What do you do for a living?' seem so irrelevant. The connection between the four of us was from the heart and there was no room for egos.

How do you express your gratitude to strangers who are willing to give unconditionally? My only insight is that the Divine knows when to send us Angels to hold our hands when the road ahead seems too long and too hard.

I trusted that the Divine would answer these prayers.

This prayer group played an amazing role, not only in my healing process, but also in restoring my faith in humanity. There are still good people in this world. We just need to open ourselves to the experience, ask for help and the Divine will send them to us.

I know that the Divine will bless this prayer group and I am forever grateful that they crossed my path – grateful that I could walk this road with them.

Acknowledgements

Heartfelt thanks to:

- God and my Guardian Angels for your incredible guidance, love and support.
- My husband Jeff, for his unconditional love, support and encouragement to always dream big.
- All the doctors and medical staff who were my pillars of hope when I could see no future.
- All my friends and colleagues all over the world, who believed in me, prayed for me and supported me during the challenging times.
- Charlotte for her unsinkable faith and prayers.
- Gaya for being a true guardian angel who still kicks my butt whenever I stop dreaming and believing.
- My dear friend, Anna, who called me every day. We share a soul sister connection.
- My family, for travelling without hesitation to support me.

- Martie, who was prepared to walk the unknown path with me.
- The incredible support staff that brightened every dark day; Chris the taxi driver, Di my house assistant, my hairdresser for making me look sexy without hair, and too many others to mention.
- Riana, who inspired me to finalize the book and publish it.
- Cyntha and Annie for your beautiful and authentic testimonials.
- Tim Hing for his incredible creative talents and for an amazing cover design.
- And lastly, all the four-legged equine animals who have touched, healed and changed my life forever.

A UNIQUE EQUINE LEADERSHIP PROGRAMME. FROM THE PADDOCK TO THE BOARD ROOM.

Chloé
CONSULTANTS

Chloe Consultants was founded by Yolanda Sing, a Senior Human Resource Executive who has worked extensively and internationally in 15 different countries.

The company specializes in:

C - *Coaching*
H - *Human Resource Consulting*
L - *Leadership Development*
O - *Organizational Development*
E - *Equine Assisted Learning*

Yolanda is a professional coach who inspires people to connect with the latent leadership qualities within themselves. Her technique is a catalyst that allows people to take charge of their lives, to find their purpose, and to draw upon their own gifts and talents to become their authentic selves.

Yolanda Sing holds four degrees specializing in People Development, Business Administration, Leadership Development and Psychology. She has spent time in Spain, USA, and Europe to qualify herself as an Equine Assisted Learning Facilitator.

Although Yolanda is based in Maclear in the Eastern Cape, South Africa, she personally runs her programmes in various centres around the country: Maclear, Johannesburg, Cape Town, Durban and Port Elizabeth as well as outside South Africa: United Kingdom, Dubai, India and Kenya.

Her programmes offer powerful and unique approaches to personal and leadership development. She applies absolute passion and global experience to all her programmes, and boasts a proven track record.

WHAT IS EQUINE ASSISTED LEARNING?

Equine Assisted Learning is an emerging field in which the horse acts as a non-judgemental partner and reflects what transpires during the process where the participant and the horse work together.
An often - used term to describe this process is 'horse whispering' – nothing mystical or mysterious at all, just simple, effective, consistent and clear communication.

No horse riding experience is required, nor is any horse riding involved. All activities are conducted on the ground.

The Equine Leadership Programme is a two-day experiential learning experience that provides a variety of leadership and team building activities.

Learning with horses helps build and strengthen;
• leadership skills • self-awareness • problem-solving and conflict resolution • anger management • ability to set and honour boundaries and overcome blind spots and non-verbal communication.

The programme is truly a magical experience when you open your heart and mind to allow the horse to guide you to a new understanding of the world you have to cope with as a Leader.

Leadership is earned through demonstrating authenticity and truthfulness and not through positional power!

WHY HORSES?

Horses are amazingly wise, clever and proud animals. Their nature is such that they live the values that organizations strive for; values which leaders try, with great difficulty, and often with little success, to instill in the hearts and minds of their employees. The old adage "direct from the horse's mouth" applies in this process – horses don't lie, and you cannot lie to them. Status does not impress them and they will reward any person that treats them with respect. Interaction with a horse touches one's emotions – be it fear, excitement or confidence. The horse provides the conduit for individual exploration as the horse provides immediate feedback and offers opportunities for profound personal growth.

- Working with a horse offers an emotional attachment that mirrors situations similar to those in which a participant may face in the workplace.
- The horse becomes a partner in the learning journey.
- Accomplishing a task involving a horse provides a wonderful metaphor when dealing with other intimidating situations in life.
- Horses are intuitive animals. They respond instinctively and are unburdened by the veneer of civility of humans.
- As herd animals they are attuned to the slightest inconsistency in their environment.

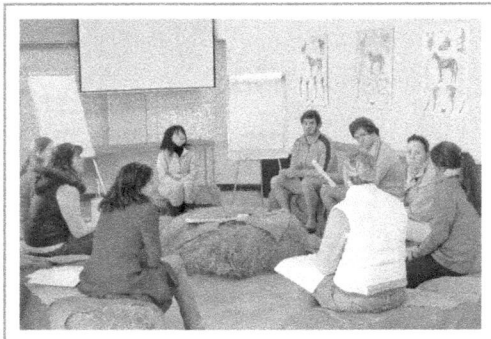

- Learning is less threatening because it is a more personal experience and feedback is direct "from the horse's mouth."
- Horses mirror human body language and emotions. We become aware of the unconscious signals we send out into the world.
- Horses are honest – you cannot fool them.
- Horses are large and powerful animals – they provide a natural opportunity to overcome fear and develop self- confidence.
- Horses are very much like humans in that they are social animals with defined roles within their herd.
- Humans can be both predatory or prey in behaviour, whereas horses carry the mindset of one that is preyed upon.

UK HR AWARD FOR BEST IN
November 2011
Award
The programme is
part of a learning
intervention
LEARNING & DEVELOPMENT

THE RESULTS

WHAT MAKES THIS PROGRAMME DIFFERENT?

- Discover true leadership capabilities with both Leadership and Emotional Intelligence focus.
- Receive unedited insights as to your natural leadership tendencies.
- Identify your comfort level in dealing with powerful followers through positive influence.
- Learn how guiding with empathy earns respect and authority.
- Pre- and Post- Emotional Intelligence Assessments.
- A Personalised Leadership Development Action Plan.

- On the spot learning takes place.
- Impact and Learning are more powerful than the traditional method of class room training.
- Participants are taken out of their comfort zones and so are more open to the process of self discovery.
- Participants are more willing to accept feedback from a Horse than from another Human Being!
- Participants see themselves and their teams from a different perspective.

ALSO AVAILABLE: EQUINE FEMALE PROGRAMMES

Learn the principles of leadership in a unique and honest environment. Experience a customized Authentic Leadership Workshop exclusively for women.

The workshop will focus on the actions needed to achieve the results each individual is striving for. Enabling the delegate to let go of the day-to-day boundaries and learn how to say "yes" when they want to and "no" when they mean it - with no guilt. Delegates will see their deepest needs reflected in the eyes of the horse.

INTERNATIONAL PROGRAMMES

SOUTH AFRICA

KENYA

UNITED KINGDOM

UNITED ARAB EMIRATES

INDIA

WHO SHOULD ATTEND THE PROGRAMME?

- Middle to Senior Management.
- The programme can be custom designed for:
  - Entry Level Management.
  - Natural working teams.
  - Female Leadership.

For further information on all programmes and bookings visit www.chloeinsa.co.za

Or contact:
Yolanda Sing
Mobile: +27(0) 71 268 6377
Email: chloeinsa@gmail.com

chloé
CONSULTANTS PTY LTD

www.ingramcontent.com/pod-product-compliance
Lightning Source LLC
Chambersburg PA
CBHW021342090426
42742CB00008B/712